I0472348

How to Start Series:

Manager or Minion?

Little's Books of Business

Ellen Onieal Little

ISBN-13: 978-1492192428
ISBN-10: 1492192422

:

DEDICATION

To all of those people who have been hardened by the economy; disappointed by the downsizing; and those whose confidence has been shot – this is for you. You just need a big sister to help you and tell you that everything will be okay. You also may need a "chin-up soldier", this is no time to be meek.

Don't let anyone tell you that "You can't"

CONTENTS

ACKNOWLEDGMENTS

I have been knocking around the idea of publishing some books since the 80s and I never had the patience or the time. I realized, through the help of my family and some unbelievably good friends that anything that I decided to do, that I should do.

First, I would like to thank my husband Wayne for his undying love and support over the last 25 years, every day it gets better. To my family; the Onieal clan all over the U.S, the Little's, Peczynski's and Ahern's from Connecticut, The Atamian's, McNew's, Bonelli's and Kweller's, I love you all.

Thank you to all the people that have been in my mastermind groups. To my clients, my colleagues, business partners and friends, without you I would not have had the confidence to do something like this.

Finally, my faith and my belief that I am always being cared for by our Heavenly Father has given me the courage to follow my heart.

Minion is defined as (by the dictionary, not Disney®)
1. An obsequious follower. **2.** A subordinate official,
especially a proud one. **3.** One who is highly esteemed or
favored; a darling. By my definition, I think of a minion as
a loyal servant, which is what you are when you are serving
others through a business or services that you provide.

Namaste.

1 THE SCIENCE OF BUSINESS

Congratulations on continuing your journey to opening your business, becoming self-employed or just learning how to be a better employee. By the way, that is our choice, do we want to be an employee or an employer?

Putting things in perspective, if we are intending on being self-employed we still become employees of the company that we created. In your own company you can either be the Manager or the Minion.

Simply put, if you are a manager you are working ON your business. If you are minion, you are working IN your business. Either is fine, but just understand, in order to grow, someone needs to be the manager. Someone needs to guide the ship.

In order to grow there needs to be a minion; a minion with a skill, talent or ability that is the solution to your target market's problem. Here we are back to the old "what came first, the chicken or the egg?", What comes first the Manager or the Minion?

Make no mistake the Manager has to come first. If you are a team of one, your manager is the business plan that you wrote. The manager is actually the mission statement of what you will do with this company. It can be simply the set of expectations that were derived in the first book of the series, Mindset over Matter.

Let's address if you are an employee and just want to get the promotion, make a better contribution, secure your employment – if you want to grow with the company, you need to know the vision, the expectations and how you can add value or contribute to the organization. To achieve a goal, I certainly need to know what the goal is.

When you are opening your own company you need the vision and the expectations on how your company will operate and eventually grow. It is so much easier to create this plan in the early stages of your business.

In Mindset over Matter we discussed putting your team on paper; who would do what; and how they would need to perform. I hope that you did that exercise. I did explain, that even if you don't have names; put in characteristics of the person who needs to fill that job or responsibility.

To increase your effectiveness an employee work with your team with this same concept. What expectations could be implemented to benefit everyone. Fill in the characteristics of the team and the team members. The best part about team projects is the respect and camaraderie of being a part of a team and self-correcting to benefit the project.

The question still remains, are you a manager or a minion. The next step above manager is CEO. All three of these positions have a different role. I also classify the Minion as self-employed; the Manager as a small business owner;

and the CEO as an Entrepreneur.

Minions should be responsible for the scopes of work, balancing responsibilities and deadlines, customer service, skill development, efficiency and safety standards.

A Manager's should be responsible for operations. Profit and Loss, maintenance of a good working environment, customer complaint resolution, community relations and networking.

A CEOs should be responsible for vision, company growth, proposing and securing contracts, communication with the operating board on budgetary needs The CEO is also responsible for joint ventures, partnerships and intellectual property compliance.

If you are an employee for someone or a manager for a corporation, you will have to replace these words, with more applicable titles for you. The responsibilities are very similar.

After reviewing this list, as a new or potentially new business owner, are you saying "I have to do all of those things"? Maybe you do; maybe you don't. In this book we are going to address all of these roles and how you can leverage and make all of these roles work in your schedule until your first growth spurt. You will also be able to identify who your first hire needs to be.

This is one of the first steps of the Science of Business. You have all these pieces to a puzzle; putting the pieces together in a synergistic, purposeful manner will create a great foundation for long term sustainability and profitability.

This basic beginning concept, is important enough, that I

am going to suggest that you not go any further in your process without figuring this out. This is the first ingredient in the Science of Business.

If you are the same person operating these three responsibilities, here is what I suggest. So, put yourself in all three of these roles:

If the minion(s) is/are good – and they are effective at their responsibilities and deadlines the manager only has to work 5 hours a week. The manger should be making follow up calls and bookkeeping duties.

If the minions are good, they are communicating how much work they can handle in their schedules and setting expectations correctly with the customers. Minions should be working 30 hours a week.

If the managers and the minions are good, the CEO has a great product to push. The CEO needs to spend 2 hours per day (10 hours per week) in exploring new ways to do business to maximize efficiency and increase partnership or venture opportunities.

Forty-five hours would be a minimum to start. You may find yourself working 60 hours. Choose where those hours are being spent, so you are alerted to what may be an opportunity in your business.

If you are spending time being a Minion: are you taking on too much work? Do you need to hire someone? Are you efficient? Organized? Well skilled at what you are doing?

If you are spending time in manager mode: again identify why? Is it time to hire? You get the idea. When you are all three roles in your business, divide your time up appropriately. If one "role" is taking you more time than is allotted, then you need to do some investigation.

This is such an easy concept, but easy to overlook. I've seen clients color code their schedules based on what activity they thought they were doing, and measured what was happening.

In this chapter, please review the responsibilities of these roles in your business world. What does each need to do to add contribution to your organization. Measure the success of each role, and identify opportunities.

☐ Minion

☐ Manager

☐ CEO

Let's draft out a mini schedule:

Sunday 2 hours Manager: Set up schedule for week log expenses and receipts.

Monday thru Wednesday: CEO 2 hours morning, setting day intentions and vision. Call for meetings with city officials, business partners, etc. Minions work 10-5 w one hour lunch.

Thursday: Manager 2 hours: invoicing and calling for appointments/purchases for next week. CEO 2 hours morning, setting day intentions and vision – product development. Minions 10-5 with one hour lunch.

Friday: CEO 2 hours morning setting day intentions and vision – follow up. Manager 1 hour networking event. Minions 10-5 with one hour lunch.

Saturday and Sunday: CEO attends Networking event.

The action item here is to fill in your schedule and stick to it. If you are a service business the Minion is working on services. Map how the efficiency is of the services.

This process will help you create the great base for your business experiment, the science of business. When you create immediate understanding what you do, you are least likely to get off track, and you will reach a level of success much quicker.

2 WHO ARE YOU?

This is not a spiritual or a trick question. You hope that your friends and the people that refer you know exactly what how to answer this question.

Very simply, ask your friends, hey do you know what I do for a living? Your friend should be able to articulate relatively easily what your services. Make sure your friends know what kind of customers you are looking for.

Since the title of this book is "Manager or Minion", I would like to stick to just defining yourself in your business as the manager or the minion, and what each role is. This eventually will also help you define who YOU really are in business – you know the Mission and Value Statement. That will be covered in the future book "Value Your Mission".

Manager or Minion? If you are the minion behind this business, the one who makes it all happen; the one that if your service was not provided the business would not be – you have a different process to follow.
As a minion it's okay to be shy and have a tough time talking to people. You just have to be able to communicate

on your team.

Author, Jim Collins book "Good to Great" makes a great illustration of this role, it's the hedgehog principle. Hedgehogs do one or two things really well, it is best illustrated by those who do what they are passionate about, they have the skill to perform their passion and they can make money doing it.

If you define yourself as the Manager (or the CEO) you have to be the visionary. You have to be responsible for creating where the company is going, how to get future clients, networking, marketing and living true to the Mission statement.

Here is another way to look at it. When I was the Manager in my business. I got more sleep. When I was the Minion (without a manager) I never slept; I was a machine. A constant hamster wheel of networking, getting clients, service, follow up, networking, repeat. It was non-stop.

If you are not a good manager, the manager role may be filled by a great Administrative Assistant, Personal Assistant, Virtual Assistant or Executive Assistant. Your choice, and define them like you want to define them. Those roles are all different to all of us. Just so you know, they are different.

As a Minion in your business, hiring is another challenge. Finding people that will replicate your brand and the quality service that you provide is one of the hardest things in business. Plus if you are doing all the work, how do you have time to hire people?

This is why we talk about all of this early on, so that you have the plan drawn out, and the surprises are really surprises and not things you just didn't plan for. Big

Difference.

Any emergencies should be evaluated after the "solve"; could this have been prevented, and whose role was it that broke down- maybe that is the person you need to hire.

In this chapter we reviewed, if you are challenged to be "the everything" in your business - come up with alternatives to each role: the Minions (production team), or the Manager (Operations)

This is also the time to use your mastermind group, mentors, your networking contacts and other resources that have been mentioned in the other series of these books, like SBA, SBDC, SCORE, EDC and the like for solutions.

Remember that every problem has a solution, and the more questions you ask, the better chance you have to solving them.

3 MINION OF THE MONTH

You can make due in your business for a while with performing as the minion. As a matter of fact, for the ease of things you my intend on just being a one person show for the duration of your business. That is perfectly fine, I know a lot of self-employed people who do just that. They have the talent, skill or ability that IS the business, and it cannot be (or you don't want it to be) replicated.

Just to make sure we are on the same wavelength, a **Minion** is defined as (by the dictionary, not Disney®) **1.** An obsequious follower. **2.** A subordinate official, especially a proud one. **3.** One who is highly esteemed or favored; a darling. By my definition, I think of a minion as a loyal servant, which is what you are when you are serving others through a business or services that you provide.

What does it mean to be the Minion in your business? Think about it. As you develop your business, as we spoke about in the first book, Mindset over Matter, you have to develop your business from the customer's point of view. You may have a skill, talent or ability – how do your customers perceive it? How do your customers want to be serviced? How do they want to be communicated to? I learned a while ago, as we were slipping out of Gorilla Marketing and into Relationship marketing that ROI no longer necessarily means Return on Investment – although it is still a very important business formula to understand.

The NEW ROI is all about Return on Impression. There are 4 or 5 pieces to the Return on Impression significance, however, the most important for these steps is How do people perceive your business from sight: your logo, your brand, your look, your first impression that you show up to a meeting in the best power outfit, etc. The second is what others' perception of your business is. What are people saying about your business, your professionalism, your location and your look.

When you start looking at your business and your service from other people's perspectives, you start gaining knowledge about what they want from you. You start creating a fan base, just like movie stars, rock stars and business professionals that you idolize. This is an exercise in putting a big mirror in your face, and realizing that feedback is your friend.

When you start getting feedback, you may be resistant to the sounds of someone else telling you that they don't like something, or that you should change something. You have to weed out the good feedback from the bad feedback. If someone tells you to dress better, or that you do not have the professional look that you should have – YOU have to ultimately decide if that is the branding you are going for. If your "feel" in your company is that you are laid back, hometown professional – the "dress down" look might be exactly what your company look should be.

On the other hand, if you are an executive professional, you should also look the part – you should always look the part based on how you want to be known, and what you want to be known for People want to spend money with whom they like and trust, you can achieve that no matter what you are wearing.

When you are a Minion in your business, you also don't have to set a standard with others. When you start working with others, you will want to set a standard that is easily understandable. Not that the standard has to be a uniform, it just has to be a uniform**ed** look.

Another detail a Minion should be aware of is your vehicle. Remember everything is an extension of you when you are in your own company. If you are a company of one, then you carry the entire brand of your company on your shoulders. If you have a mess in your vehicle, hide it in your trunk, make sure your first impression with your customers is a good one.

A clean vehicle speaks organization, care and consideration.   This also includes driving habits. If you decide to use marketing material (like car magnets) on your vehicle, then by all means, make sure the vehicle is clean and that you leave your road rage at the house or office.

This book is not really a checklist like the others, but we did cover quite a bit in this chapter.

Be the best YOU you can be. Brand yourself with excellence – Give Value to your clients.

Develop your business from the customers (target market) point of view to make sure you are hitting the marks, and cultivating that Solution to their problem effectively.

Pay attention to your Return on Impression. This is why I have not discussed marketing yet. In this stage you are developing "off line" who you are online with images and services – so that when we talk about your online presence with your website and your social media you are hitting your target market where they are, and with the right "stuff" to make you memorable, relatable and referable.

Lastly, if you decide to remain the minion of your business, then you can consider yourself self-employed. It should give you the direction on how to incorporate your business, and also absolve you from managing others. I still suggest that you make sure you bring on a bookkeeper. Being self-employed is very rewarding and you can certainly position the business for sale as long as you can find someone to replicate the product or service you are selling.

4 MANAGER OF CHOICE

Once you have decided to become the Manager of your business, you will vacillate as to whether you just want to remain a Minion. The "middle" management position in any corporation that I ever worked for was the worst job of them all! As the manager, at times, you will say, "it's just easier if I do it" or "I do it better" – remind yourself of this chapter when that time comes. It is worth it when you move yourself into managing your business, rather than just working AS your business. So how does it all get done? Friends, it's easier and harder than you think.

First, you have to hire who will do the service or the sales of your product. The Minion of your business is the Production team. Production team is responsible for delivering quality products or services in the expected time frame. You may be the "courteous service" part as the manager.

Once you hire this person (and it could be a partner, by the way), you both have to manage expectations. Remember as we define these roles, it's not that one person is the "boss" of another person: in a small business everyone is on the same team, and the team can self-correct if this is done right. Set the expectations of what needs to be done, how it needs to be completed and in what time frame. As the manager, it is also your responsibility to manage the work load. You need to know how much 1 properly trained person can produce, in order to have a measurement of future hires. Furthermore, it is prudent for you to know, and to allow the Production team to hire the next hire – the production team currently becomes the production team leader, and so the company grows.

As the manager you are the sales, marketing and operations team. If you are not able to manage the bookkeeping part of the business, it is much easier to hire people sooner than later for your financing "chores". If you start with someone early, it is less money in the long run. In the previous chapter we discussed a mock weekly schedule for the manager if you were filling all three roles: Minion, Manager and CEO:

- ☐ Sunday 2 hours Manager: Set up schedule for week. Log expenses and receipts

- ☐ Thursday: Manager 2 hours: invoicing and calling for appointments/purchases for next week

- ☐ Friday: Manager 1 hour networking event.

If you have a production team, this is what the manager schedule should look like:

- ☐ Sunday 2 hours Manager: Set up schedule for week log expenses and receipts

- ☐ Monday: follow up on sales calls send out weekly

newsletter and email campaign: Strategy Session call/meeting

- ☐ Tuesday: Sales Follow up on emails that went out 3 hours, Production team help 4 hours.

- ☐ Wednesday: Sales and Networking 2 hours; update website and mailing lists.

- ☐ Thursday: Manager 2 hours: invoicing and calling for appointments/purchases/sales for next week

- ☐ Friday Manager Sales and 1 hour networking event. 4 hours Production team help.

- ☐ Through this you may also be answering phones, client satisfaction issues and more.

By helping the production team, you will see processes and how to maximize efficiency. You will also be determining how much time it takes for each service or product to be completed.

The manager should hire the operations team. Your very first hire should be in bookkeeping, again, even if you are all three roles to your business.

Your second hire should be Sales team, and the third hire should be an administrative assistant. Then and only then are you ready to be the CEO. I always say, if you are going to be something, you may as well be the best. How about being the CEO of the Universe??

5 CEO OF THE UNIVERSE

As the CEO, which technically you always have been at some level. You are the CEO for YOU for sure. It's kind of silly to say the CEO of the Universe, however there is a reason why I say that. CEOs are rarely revered. Take Steve Jobs for instance, God Rest his soul. He was a self-proclaimed ass. Everyone that worked for him directly spoke about how ruthless he was in his words and actions. He was a great CEO for what he did for the company.

The CEO of General Electric, Jack Welch; not hated, but certainly not known for his warm personality. He was a numbers guy. He believed there is always a bottom 10%, and every year, you hack off the bottom 10%. Bob Nardelli, Mr Welch's protégé, did the same when he became CEO of Home Depot.

We are now talking about YOUR business. You can be the CEO of the universe. The CEO that makes a difference, the CEO that brings growth to your company; that increases their value to the community. You get to write this chapter, on what type of CEO you will be.

What does it mean to act like a CEO? What does it mean to perform like a CEO? What do CEO's think like?

I have been studying CEOs for years. They are visionaries and decision makers. They are profoundly intense in their time management and rarely mince words when it comes to business. The business is a machine that either works or it doesn't, that either profits or loses; that either stands out or just survives – or worse, closes up.

There is no emotion with the job of CEO, you need to do what is right for the machine. In order t make those decisions you need non-emotional reporting that can tell you the health and the well-being of your organization. As the CEO you are the face of the organization with the players that can take your company to new heights

Each month your operations team should be reporting to you through your managers and team leaders. You need to make sure as the CEO that you do not cross the lines over to the production team or the operations team, so not to overstep your bounds and to minimize the capabilities of the managers you have in place. These are the types of things that will make you CEO of the universe!

Lastly as the CEO, you need to be constantly striving for growth in a manageable sustained rate. You are responsible for contracts, new business and budget responsibilities. As the CEO, you should create a board for your company. Call it your strategy or your mastermind group if you would like, that is responsible for keeping you on the growth strategy plan and manage the course along the way.

6 WORKING TOGETHER

Working together as a well-oiled machine is just as important as it sounds. Hopefully I have given you an illustration on how to keep your executive team on course for success. It sounds easy, however the execution of this is most times a FAIL. You will never understand the importance of communication until you have been miscommunicated or communicated to poorly. It can cost you and your company time, money and energy. This is the longest part of the book because it is the most important.

There is a really important dynamic in this book that you may not be catching so I want to make sure it's clear. Call everyone something on your team. I used to use lieutenants, captains, team captains, shift leaders, masters of____, whatever seemed to fit the bill, and that didn't sound condescending. Everyone has a need to contribute. To a startup company everyone should be "founders" or "charter members". Once everyone has a role, it will be easier to define what the expectations are for that role, and then the lines of communication are easier.

With new business, I call it the "a customer calls" process.

What happens in your company when a customer calls. It should go something like this: The Admin. Passes the info off to the sales team, who collects the money and gives it to the bookkeeper. Once the bookkeeper verifies funds, they notify the sales team, who notifies production. Production gives sales team estimated time of completion, the sales team calls back the customer with a follow up call thanking them for their business and discloses the estimated time of delivery plus 2 days.

Meanwhile, Operations manager gets feedback from Production team and notifies sales team if any delays are going to happen within 48 hours of expected completion time stated by Production team. Production team finishes product, Sales team delivers product early, and then sends out a thank you note for business, and a call to action for referral or future business. Sales team does 90 day follow up, again with an call to action for referral or future business, and the process is complete.

The marketing team gets testimonial from customer which goes on marketing material (with permission) and puts customer on a drip email campaign which goes out a minimum of once per month reminding the customer of any promotions or new business options.

In small businesses, it is imperative that you have a process like this so that you know when something goes wrong, where it broke in the process. Each player on the team needs to know what their role in in the process, the easiest mode of communication and expected response times. When I say mode of communication, we are in the age, that you may be employing virtual people. (not really virtual people; people that are not physically with you), modes of communication may be text, e-mail, voice mail, video mail, skype, google hangout and phone.

The best way to manage all of this is weekly meetings with the leaders of the groups to understand what business is currently happening, what new business you need and what the budgets are. Managing this as a weekly process is so critical to your success and long term retain-ability and sustainability. The retention for your employees and the sustaining for your profits.

So, this just sounds like one big happy family, right? Well, conflict will happen my friends. It is inevitable. Well, if your people are worth their weight in gold, there will be conflict. Conflict is a great growth engine, it's like gas with octane in it.

If you put octane in a 1960 Rabbit, I'm sure it will not run well When you have the right people on your team, you are no longer the 1960 Rabbitt, you'll be the super-fast race car. In the super-fast, super-cool race car, octane can be the boost that your team needs to get through glass ceilings of achievement, rough spots and new adventures. Any time there is conflict or change, there is usually not one without the other.

How do you manage conflict then? First, set the rules early about disagreements, how they will be handled and what the venue is. You should, while there is NO conflict, discuss as a team how you will handle conflict and make sure the team agrees and follows through with the process.

For instance, my first rule of conflict is that the team handles it within their realm first. Using the production team as an example, if someone is not performing on the production team, another team member should be the first to rectify the problem, retrain the employee or ask for help.

The second rule of conflict should be a simple one, there is no yelling or pointing of fingers. I know this may sound like school yard antics, however you would be surprised. My motto has always been "When emotions are high, intelligence is low". If someone is that heated in a conflict, it is best to get them to a manageable state first, before addressing the problem.

Third Rule of conflict, the rules according to Ellen, is that every problem has a solution. In conflict situations, sometimes the conflict is resolved by compromise; and a compromise is a solution. More importantly, you need to make sure that both sides are heard, and that there is a mediator. In your "rule setting" make sure you have a mediator named for these instances.

Fourth rule; all resolutions are made and decided upon for the betterment of the company not the individual. If the individual wins, the company does not. The individual will always win in the long term, if the company is always in the best interest in any conflict.

Fifth rule: all conflict situations are handled in private, involving the people who need to know and can fix the situation. All attendees must be the "problem solvers" not the "problem finders".

Sixth and last, and most important. Question don't judge; and question a lot. Don't always know the answer either. In fact, it's best NOT to know all the answers. You may be surprised with the other options that arise!

In one of the companies I started as an adult, my partner and I did not come up with the "how to resolve" piece. She and I made rules, but then did not have a plan to talk about the breaking or bending of rules when they happened. This particular business was a food industry business, and we agreed that no free food to anyone, unless it was customer satisfaction. If we wanted to eat there, we paid full price. We set that rule for the first 6 months. Within 3 months, she was eating lunch there every day AND feeding her family on OUR profits. I was incensed. Since we had no real conflict resolution plan, I blew up. My husband was not eating there for free. I was not eating there for free, what made her think that she could. Needless to say, the conflict enveloped our relationship. Eventually, the store closed; and although a very stressful process – I was relieved. It was the ultimate resolution to our conflict. I don't want that to happen to anyone else. <that was a great business>.

Other conflicts that happened in other companies we had involved bookkeeping. I remember getting my husband's pay sheets on napkins, because of the inefficiency of the bookkeeper – messed our taxes up for months. Time wasters like position of furniture and what wholesaler to use; you can imagine a million things could go wrong.

That is the best way to start this conversation. Not only is it a great mastermind tool, but it keeps everyone on their toes. "Let's Brainstorm what could possibly go wrong in our business!". I certainly wouldn't call it a "pep" talk – you can imagine – maybe you have this meeting over a company purchased lunch.

What happens when you ask that question? You start coming up with some obstacles that you can overcome. How do you know you can overcome them? Now you have time; now there is no emotion; now you have clear minded individuals that can think through process and project. Amazing right?

In fact, this is a great exercise when you are creating your business plan; which we also will discuss in an upcoming edition of the How to Start Series "Planning for Biz".

The last type of conflict that you may encounter may be unpleasant. It may be when an employee acts out of line. This is a great time to have an HR professional that you can ask questions, just to stay within your state laws. Many HR professionals have consulting businesses, you can certainly consult your local SHRM organization in your area for the best of the best.

This is your business. Please do not involve yourself in pettiness, name calling, poor behavior, disrespectful employees, road rage, poor social media posts, you know what I am talking about. And if you are the manager and CEO of your business with employees, do not deal with employees back talking you, being disrespectful, or involving your customers in drama. None of this behavior should be tolerated. This is the face of your company, and how you are treated is just as important as anything. Another famous phrase "how you do ONE thing, is how you do EVERYTHING". If your employees are acting poorly, that is not conflict resolution, that is employee action time.

Let's review the process. First you are going to decide what your role is in the business. Are you the Minion, the Manager or the CEO?

Whichever you choose, you are going to plan out how you grow the company with you in each of the roles. Remember, do not measure yourself by someone else's yardstick, you plan out your success, your way – so that it is manageable, sustainable and you will be able to enjoy the process.

You are going to set expectations for each role, department and activity. Make sure you have meetings weekly to challenge each other, and grow as a team.

Decide on how you will manage conflict before it happens. Don't know the answers to all the questions, let the team solve whatever situations can be solved by the team.

There are 2 or 3 more books to consider before you officially open your business. You've read "Mindset over Matter", you now know that you have the resources that you need to accomplish this.

In this book, you set your expectations for who will work with you and how you will grow. Your first hire should be whom??... right, the bookkeeper.

The next book in this series is "Finding Fans". In these first 3 books, you are developing who you are off line first, before you start developing your business in the community and online. Take your time through this process, or should I say – Stay on your time line. Keep your project moving, and stay positive. You are about to do something really great.

Action Items for this Edition:

1. Review the responsibilities of these roles in your business world. What does each need to do to add contribution to your organization.

    ☐   Minion

    ☐   Manager

    ☐   CEO

2. Draft out a mini schedule
3. Are you the Minion, the Manager or the CEO?
4. Who do you have to hire, and when will that happen, what are the thresholds for the first new hires.
5. Be the best YOU you can be. Brand yourself with excellence – Give Value to your clients.
6. Develop your business from the customers (target market) point of view to make sure you are hitting the marks, and cultivating that Solution to their problem effectively.
7. Pay attention to your Return on Impression. What your customers see and what they "hear" about you.
8. If you consider yourself self-employed. It should give you the direction on how to incorporate your business,

This section of your business development takes trust. It takes time to do it right. Your dividends will pay big if you hire the right, better yet, the BEST people for the position, not your friends that can "do the job". Also, put yourself in the best role for your talent skills and abilities.

When you decide to start hiring the best way to start is to show potential hires the expectations; usually they will tell you if they can or can't perform the items. Or they will tell you in their language, "well I could learn", startups don' t have the money to have someone learn on their dime.

People Management or human capital is the most challenging part of any business. It's all about getting the right fit, and not settling when you think you "have to" get someone. Get the "right" someone's

I can't reiterate enough how proud I am of you, the reader of this book. I made this series easy to follow for a reason, so you can get right to making a stream of income for yourself. The beginning stages take time, but they save you so much more time in the long run.

Be sure to pick up the next book in the series, "Finding Fans". You are one step closer.

You can contact me through my website:
www.HowtoStartSeries.com or
Ellen@BusinessResolutions.org.

I am on every social media channel, as Ellen Onieal Little, Business Resolutions and How to Start Series. Thank you for letting me be your guide through this great journey!

ABOUT THE AUTHOR

Ellen Onieal Little comes from a long line of Heart filled people, who have been giving back to our communities for 60 years or more. My earliest t memory of our entrepreneurial spirit was my mother. She started a Diet Control Business in New Jersey back in the early to mid-60's and was challenged by the powerhouse of Diet programs, which is still in existence today.

I don't know all the particulars, but I know that my mother didn't back down because Diet Control became a thriving business, and contributed to my Mother's tenacity and confidence. Whether or not they chose to agree or disagree, or whether they decided to co-exist; it didn't matter.

50 Years later, I must have absorbed my mother's stick-to-itiveness; her drive; her love for people – because here I am helping entrepreneurs, teaching tactical, practical applications to business practices. I have owned a coffee shop and several other businesses.

I have helped over 100 entrepreneurs; independent contractors, multi-level marketing teams and individuals create business plans, marketing plans and strategy planning sessions. I don't just teach the plan, but how to derive/arrive at the plan. I teach HOW to use the tools, not just what the tools are.

I hope you benefit from this knowledge. I spent a lifetime living it.